HORSE LOVERS FIRST BOOK

Debbie Burgermeister

Copyright © 2019

The moral right of Debbie Burgermeister to be identified as the author
and Meftahul Amin to be identified as the cover illustrator
has been asserted by them in accordance with the Copyright, Design and
Patents Act 1988.

All rights reserved. No part of this book may be reproduced or
transmitted in any form or by any means, electronic or mechanical,
including photocopying, recording, or by any information storage and
retrieval system, without permission in writing from the copyright owner,
except for the inclusion of brief quotations in a review.

 A catalogue record for this work is available from the National Library of Australia

ISBN: 9780648743705

Book creation, editing, design and layout by Crazy Diamond Publishing
Print and channel distribution: Lightning Source / Ingram
Publisher: Horse Riding Hub

www.horseridinghub.com

DISCLAIMER: "All content, including text, graphics, images and
information, contained on or available through this book is for general
information purposes only. Such information is subject to change without
notice. You are encouraged to confirm any information obtained from or
through this book with other sources and professionals."

This book is about
creating confidence and a safer path
to horse care, riding, or owning a horse one day.

Your author Debbie has a lifetime of
horsemanship experience and in-depth
knowledge to share. She has a passion for people of all
ages to learn safely. Helping people start out with the core
fundamentals to support the future of sensible,
confident and capable horse handlers and riders.

We hope you enjoy this book from an expert
who has owned, cared for and loved her horses
through many ups and downs.

The author competing in her younger years
at age 17, on her horse Queeny in a hack class.

Horse Lovers' First Book

Questions in this book

- What is the difference between a horse and a pony? 5
- What are the parts of a horse? 6
- Are horses colourful? 8
- Do horses have socks? 12
- How do I know if my horse is happy? 14
- Do horses talk? 15
- Why do horses wear shoes? 16
- How can you tell a horse's age? 18
- Do horses need grooming? 20
- What is the gait of a horse? 22
- What equipment do I need to ride a horse? 24
- How do I control a horse and what are aids? 26
- What do horses eat? 30
- How do horses sleep? 31

Are you horse crazy?

Things that you would say to yourself.

1. I own at least one toy horse
2. I love the smell of horses
3. I don't care about getting dirty
4. I would rather muck out a stall than clean my room
5. I own at least 3 books about horses
6. I make horse jumps at home out of brooms, buckets and stools
7. I dream about horses
8. I have horse pictures in my bedroom
9. I love to act like a horse trotting and galloping around
10. I could spend all day in a horse shop
11. I pretend that my bicycle is a horse
12. I love watching any type of horse movie

Horse Lovers First Book

How horse mad are you?
What was your score?

1: Try again

2-5 Mild fever

6-9: High fever

10-11: Delirium

All 12: You are certifiably horse crazy.
There is no hope for you or your parents
to be able to change.
Continue to dream big
and enjoy a life with horses.
IT'S THE BEST!!

Giddy Up Beginner Books

Horses

What's the difference between a horse and a pony?

They are the same species (Equus caballus). Measured in 'hands', a pony is less than 14.2hh (hands high). 1hand = 4inches = 10.16centimetres, measured at the withers (base of the neck) to the ground.

A smaller pony, usually 70-107cm is a Shetland Pony, and heights under 86-97cm are called a Miniature Horse, which are much finer in their bones and coat.

A male horse is called a 'Colt' up until he is three years old. At that point the name changes, and if he is castrated he is called a gelding, and cannot father babies. An ungelded horse is called a Stallion, and he can become a father.

A female horse is called a Filly until she is three, after that she is called a Mare.

Shetland Pony and Foal

What are the parts of a horse?

Horse Head.

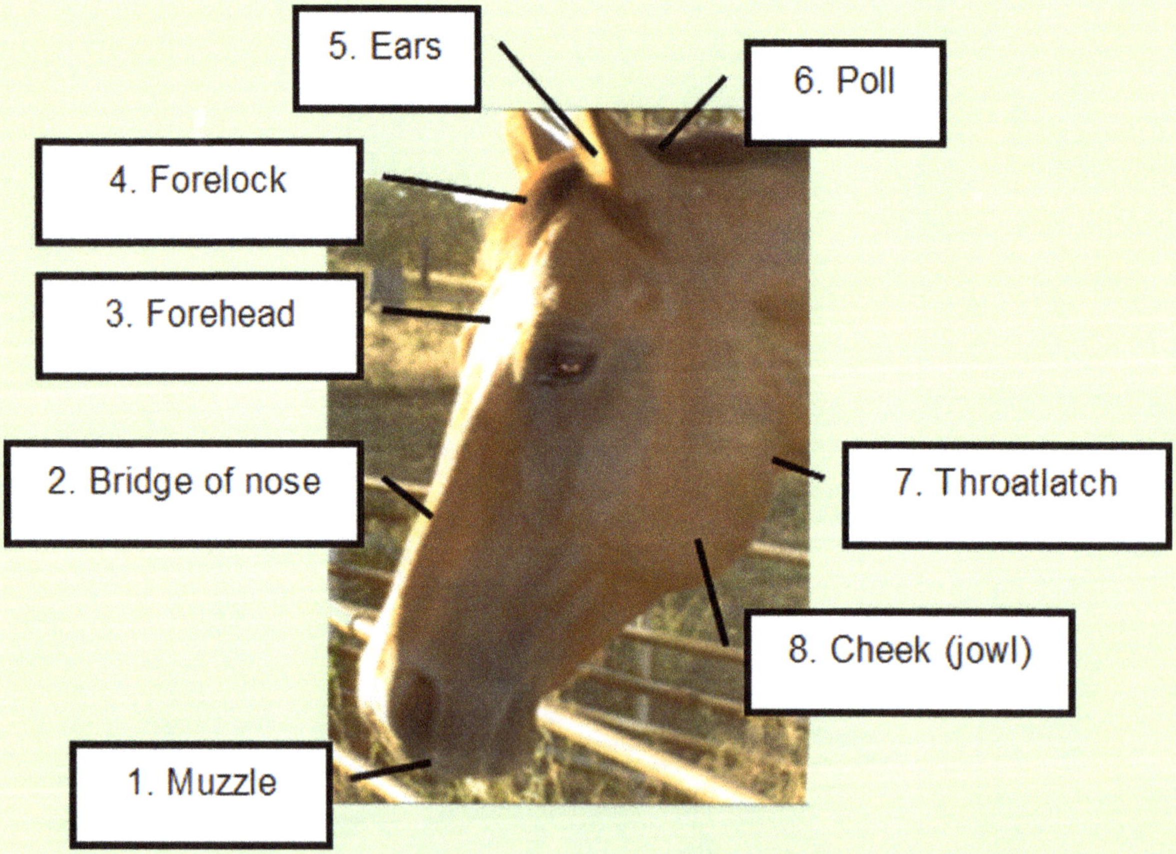

- 5. Ears
- 6. Poll
- 4. Forelock
- 3. Forehead
- 2. Bridge of nose
- 7. Throatlatch
- 8. Cheek (jowl)
- 1. Muzzle

Horse Lovers First Book

These are the parts of the body.

- 1. Hoof
- 2. Knee
- 3. Shoulder
- 4. Neck
- 5. Mane, Crest
- 6. Withers
- 7. Back
- 8. Loin
- 9. Hip
- 10. Rump
- 11. Tail
- 12. Hock
- 13. Fetlock
- 14. Coronet
- 15. Flank

Are horses colourful?

The basic colours you will see are Brown, Bay (brown with black mane and tail and usually a black strip on top of rump to tail), Black, Chestnut (red/orange with mane and tail same colour as coat), Flaxen (a lighter mane and tail), Liver Chestnut (a very dark chestnut). There are many variations of white (light grey, dapple grey or white) and flea bitten (black sprinkled through a white coat).

Other colours can be mixed with the name of a breed. Some are Cremellos (white mane and tail with pink skin), Roan (reddish and blue mix of colours with white), Palomino (golden with white mane and tail), Paint/Pinto (black and white is Piebald and brown and white is Skewbald), and Appaloosa (looks like a leopard, white with dark spots).

This type of brown is called Seal Brown.

Horse Lovers First Book

This horse is Bay.
Note the black mane and tail.

A white horse.

This colour is chestnut.

This cream-coloured horse is a Cremello.

Pinto

Appaloosa

This beautiful gold and silver horse is a Palomino.

Horse Lovers First Book

The popular breeds (types) of horses are Andalusian, Australian Stock Horse, Arab, Clydesdale, Quarter Horse, Shetland, Standardbred, Thoroughbred, Waler, Warmblood, and Welsh Pony.

An Arabian horse: Endurance and prowess, one of the most recognisable horse breeds in the world. Note the high tail, fine legs and dished nose.

A Quarter horse: Broad chest and heavy-muscled with small ears, a big jaw and short body. Very intelligent with fast speed up to a quarter of a mile.

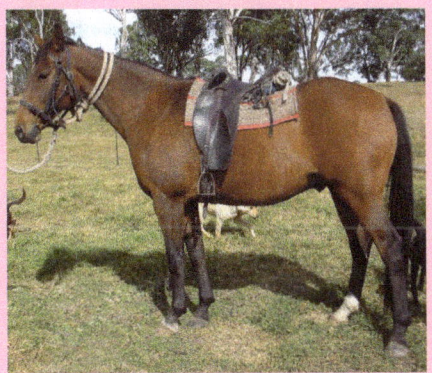

An Australian Stock horse: Versatile, hardy breed noted for endurance, agility and good temperament.

A Shetland pony: Small with short legs and a heavy coat, long thick mane, forelock and tail. Ranging in height from only 70cm to 107cm.

Do horses have socks?

You will generally see white points on a horse and they all have different terms such as:

LEGS: Coronet (small white line above hoof), Half Pastern (wide white marking above hoof), Sock (as it sounds), Stocking (like a long white sock from hoof to knee).

Coronet

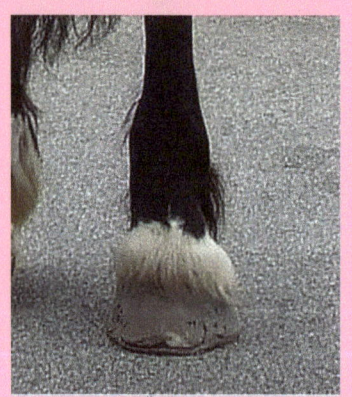

Half pastern

Socks

Stockings

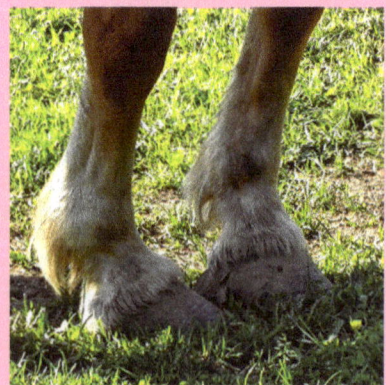

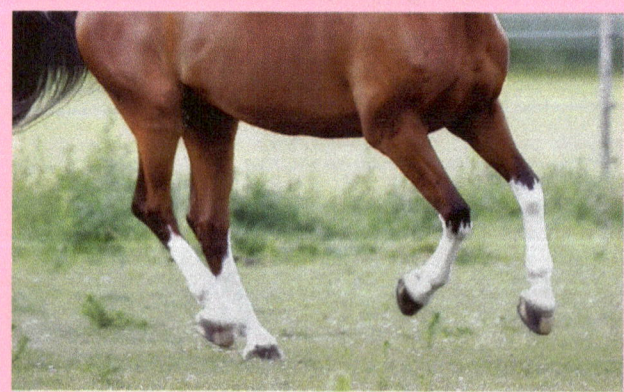

Horse Lovers First Book

FACE:
Star (between eyes), Snip (white between nostrils), Blaze (between eyes to end of nose), Bald (most front of face white), Stripe (thin white blaze like a line from eyes to nose).

Star and snip

Blaze

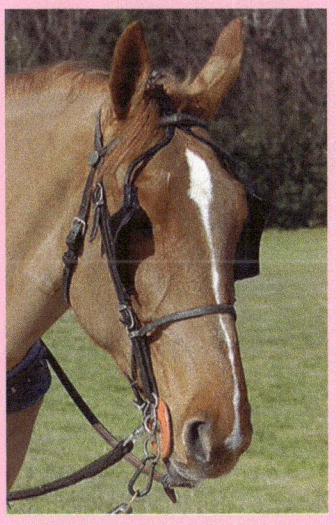

Stripe

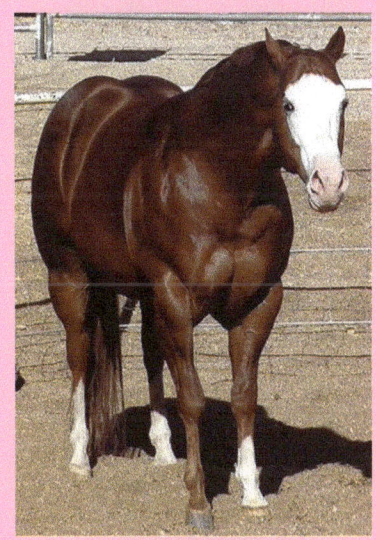

Bald

How do I know if my horse is happy?

You can tell if a horse is happy and relaxed when its ears are forward, a kind look in its eye, a relaxed low head when standing, not moving around and looking content (happy). If a horse shows the white of its eye, this indicates they are unhappy or annoyed and may be dangerous. The horse on the left is not a happy horse. Standing behind it is very dangerous!

Do horses talk?

Horses communicate with a sound called a whinny. Keen horse owners can even tell the difference between horses from their whinny. You will hear this often at feed time or talking to other horses. To communicate well with horses we must learn body language and tone of voice because they will understand how you feel and respond accordingly.

Common terms you need to know when working with horse owners:

- "Nearside" is the left and "offside" is the right when you are facing the same direction as the horse.

- "Hands" is the measure of height.

- "Squeal", "nicker", "neigh", "whinny" are all horse sounds to communicate with us and other horses.

- "Aids" are what we use when riding to tell the horse what we want to do. Natural aids are using your body to communicate. This includes tone of voice, use of hands and legs to turn, or body balance to stop and go.

- "Tack" is the gear we use to put on our horse to ride. This includes halter, bridle, reins, saddle pad and saddle.

Why do horses wear shoes?

A horse foot is called a hoof. In the sole of the hoof is a frog. This helps blood flow through the body and keep the foot healthy.

There are many different reasons why horses need shoes. If you don't have to shoe your horse, you can leave your horse barefoot. You will save yourself a lot of money.

But for high level competition, we generally need to give our horse more grip and foot shape. Getting them fit for some sports needs to be along roads or out in the bush where it can be rocky in some places. Having a stone bruise can stop your horse from being ridden for months.

Some properties are hilly and rocky so we support our horses' feet. Some horses have had shoes from a young age so their feet get sore without shoes.

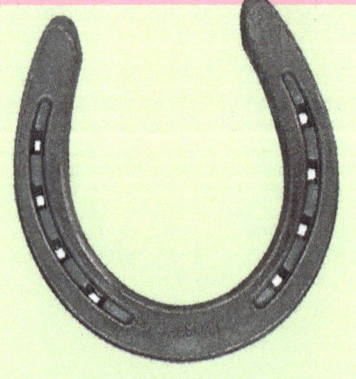
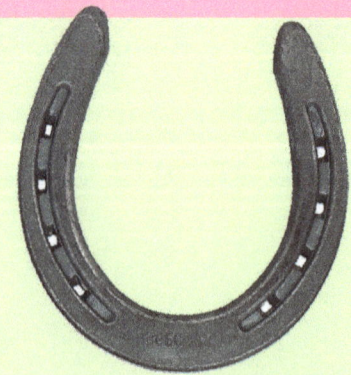

Horse Lovers First Book

How can you tell a horse's age?

A foal is under 1 and still getting milk from mum..

A weanling is under 1 and no longer getting milk from mum.

A yearling is 1-2 years old.

Filly (female) and Colt (male) are 2-3 years old.

Horse from 4yrs+.

Some horses have a "brand", which is usually two sets of numbers burnt into their coat, indicating the number of the foal and the birth year. Letters or symbols refer to the breeder or society.
  For instance, 14 over 5 looks like this: 14
                                            5

This means it is the fourteenth foal born in 1995 or 2005 or 2015. Usually the horse will show its age sufficiently to tell us which decade it would be and we can also tell by looking at the teeth.

Horse Lovers First Book

You can tell the age of this horse easily. He's very old and tired. See the dipped back, grey hair, and enlarged bones around the knee? You will sometimes start to see an old horse's ribs. The horse would have longer teeth and its joints are usually stiff. Unless an old horse over 25 is kept fit in light work with very good feed and supplements, they will naturally decline in body shape.

Giddy Up Beginner Books

Do horses need grooming?

Yes, it is important to clean the horse before you put a saddle cloth and saddle on them to ride. This ensures there are no uncomfortable burrs, dirt or loose hair that may agitate the horse when riding,

Also:

- To remove mud, sweat and old hair;
- To notice any irregularities and injuries;
- To stimulate blood flow to the skin for a healthier coat and muscle tone;
- To create a special bond with the horse.

The basic items used are a soft or dandy brush, curry comb, mane and tail brush and a hoof pick.

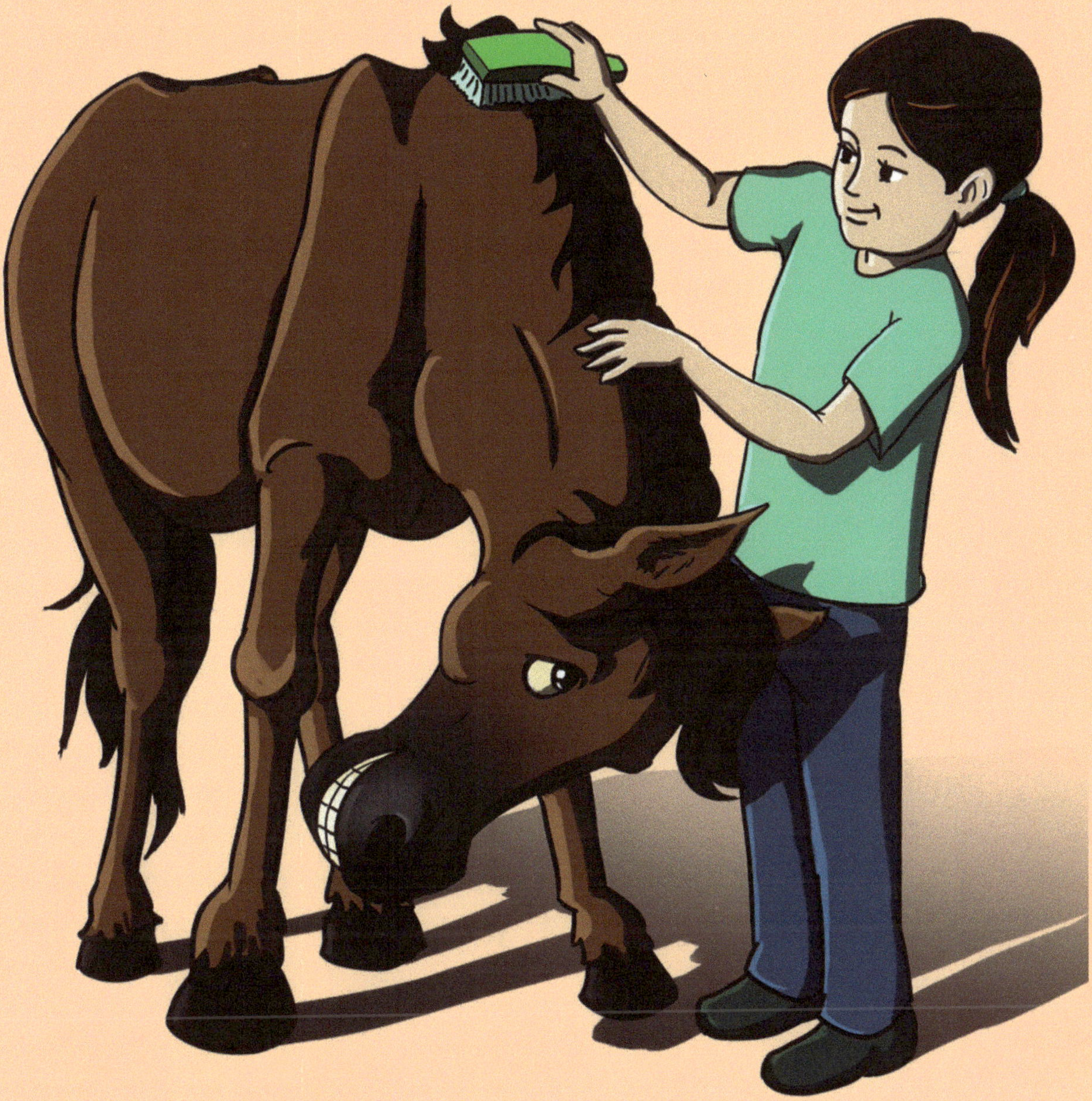

Horse Lovers First Book

What is the gait of a horse?

The word "gait" is used to describe its movement. They are either moving at a walk (slow), a trot (like jogging), a canter (like running) or a gallop (sprinting fast).

Walk (4 beat)   Trot (2 beat)   Canter (3 beat)   Gallop (4 beat)
                                Right Lead   Right Lead

When a horse backs naturally without interference from the rider, it performs a two beat diagonal gait similar to the trot. The pattern may be the right front moving with the left hind and the left front moving with the right hind.

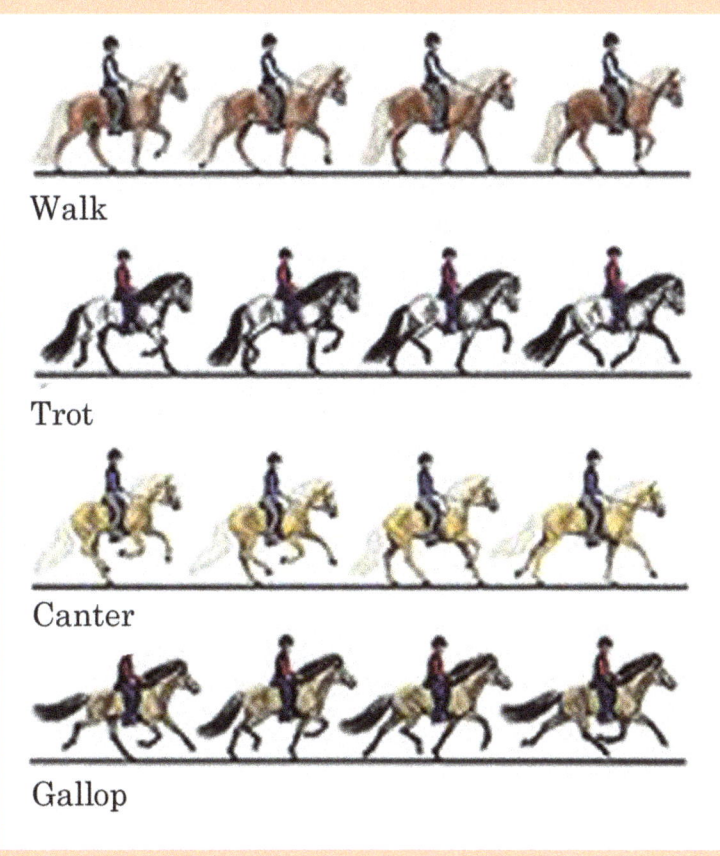

What equipment do I need to ride a horse?

For comfortable, safe and controlled riding, both the rider and horse need appropriate equipment.

RIDER GEAR

Most important for safety is an approved standard helmet – Australian (AS/NZS 3838 or ARB HS 2012 marked SAI global), American (ASTM F1163 SEI marked), British/European (PAS015 or VG1 BSI Kitemarked).

A collared shirt for the sun, jeans or jodhpurs (tights can be slippery in the saddle), boots (sneakers don't have a small heel and can be a danger falling through the stirrup).

Most riding schools supply helmets so, when starting out, long pants and boots are the most important.

HORSE GEAR

Most riding schools will supply horses and all the necessary gear, such as:

- Halter for catching the horse;
- Bridle for riding. Some bridles have a "bit" which is a metal or rubber piece that sits comfortably in the horse's mouth;
- Saddle cloth, which is like a mat to place the saddle on;
- Saddle for riding;
- Leg boots for jumping.

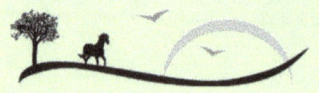

Riding Styles

There are different styles of riding depending on what you like, what equestrian sport you are involved in and the type of horse. The gear will be slightly different based on whether it is English or Western style of riding.

The core principals of riding are the same across all styles. Riders start to favour a type of riding style to be more relaxed, more precise and controlled, or more exciting. All riding disciplines have their own special qualities.

Horse Sports / Equine Disciplines

There are a large variety of horse activities to experience. These are: Pony Club, Dressage, Jumping, Cross Country, Trial Riding, Endurance, Campdrafting, Team Penning, Cutting, Polocrosse, Polo, Horse Ball, Racing, Archery, Trick Riding, Trick Training, Rodeo and Barrel Racing.

How do I control a horse and what are aids?

To have a happy horse, it's important to understand how to communicate through your body with the horse and through how you use your "aids". Natural aids include verbal communication and, most importantly, how you hold your reins with your fingers, hands and arms. How you sit in the saddle (your seat), and how you position your legs from your thigh, knee, calf of your leg, ankle and feet are also important.

Sometimes artificial 'aids' are used with a whip and spurs, but only experienced riders or riders under instruction should introduce them based on horse behaviours.

Giddy Up Beginner Books

How not to ride a horse.

Legs out, hands in the air, not holding the reins, scared and in a panic and no communication with an angry kicking horse, out of control and unsafe.

Horse Lovers First Book

How to ride a horse properly.

Sitting straight, slight bend in knee with ankles and hip in line, toes up and heels down, holding the reins with hands nice and low, in control, calm and confident with a happy horse.

What do horses eat?

Their main diet is roughage such as grass. When there is not enough grass we substitute with hay (lucerne, barley, rhodes grass), or chaff, which is finely chopped hay.

Additional grains and supplements are added depending on the weight, age and exercise of the horse. These can include barley, oats, corn, lupins and pre-mixed feeds.

How do horses sleep?

Horses can actually sleep standing up and even with their eyes open! Most of their sleeping is done this way because they have a mechanism in their legs called a "stay apparatus" allowing them to relax their muscles while keeping their legs locked in position to hold them up.

When very tired, they will sit down on a soft surface or lie down flat on their side only in short bursts for 20 minutes or up to 2 hours a day.

They love having a nice snooze in the sun on sand.

Your dream horse

My Horse's Name: _____   Age: _____

Height (in hands): _____   Weight (kg): _____

Gender: _____   Breed: _____

Colour: _____

Horse Lovers First Book

It is highly recommended to take the time to learn the basics of horse care, handling and riding preparation before stepping into the world of riding. But sometimes due to cost and time constraint this is not achievable for most without their own horse.

If there is one thing you take away from this book it should be to remember these words when starting out with horses...Please take care in your journey to learn safely with an *experienced coach* and *well trained* horse, to have a better chance of positive outcomes.

Giddy Up Beginner Books

UNTIL NEXT TIME... RIDE, RELAX, ENJOY

I wish you happiness and health always!

Learn more and feel better with equine energy!

LOVE, LAUGH, LIVE

DANCE AND SING

SHARE YOUR LIGHT

RUN FREE WITH HORSES

Debbie Burgermeister

Your Author

Your author Debbie Burgermeister – with thanks to my Mum and Dad and two brothers for blessing me with an amazing horse life and these memories. With my husband and twins we also have a new family journey with horses to enjoy.

A Life with Horses

Giddy Up Beginner Books

With thanks to the many horses that have shaped my life, blessing me with a shoulder to lean on and a best friend forever: Beauty, Gidget, Cassie, Talisa, Prince, Queeny, Mooney, Kit, Cascade, Casanova, Cassette, PK, Gabby, Jazz, Buttons, Ruby, Judge and beautiful Magic.

Horse Lovers First Book

Giddy Up Beginner Books

Horse Lovers First Book

Giddy Up Beginner Books

Create your memories
and enjoy a wonderful life with horses!

GIDDY UP BEGINNER BOOKS

Collect The Series

Easy to read for kids and adults

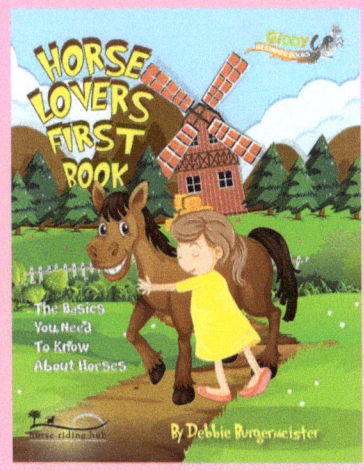

HORSE LOVERS FIRST BOOK: A first horse book filled with colour, horse cartoons, photos and answers to the very basics you need to know about horses.

HOW TO RIDE A HORSE: Riding Lessons for Beginners Workbook as a step-by-step education resource. With a bonus development guide for parents.

READY FOR YOUR FIRST HORSE?: Read this first! An expert's guide when looking for a beginner's horse for sale. Essential checklists for everything you need to find out before owning a horse.

Become A Horse Lover Member!

Find out how at
www.horseridinghub.com/membershub

AN EDUCATION PATHWAY

Horse Lovers Worldwide

Horses are our heritage! Help keep horses a part of our community, to run free with these amazing animals. Experience the joy and freedom they bring into your life and the lives of those around you.

A resource for beginner horse lovers to obtain quality information and education for a safer horse journey.

www.ingramcontent.com/pod-product-compliance
Lightning Source LLC
Chambersburg PA
CBHW061816290426
44110CB00026B/2884